I0393952

Mortgage Management For The Single Daddy

How To Save Money By Managing Your
Mortgage Payments Better

Nick Thomas

Visit my website at www.singledaddydating.com

ISBN-13: 978-1505405514

ISBN-10: 1505405513

JOIN OUR COMMUNITY!

Single Daddy Dating is a growing community of single fathers who look to help each other, not only with dating success but in all areas of their lives too. This includes parenting, career and finances advice.

Join us today and get '**10 Crucial Checklist To Dating Success For Single Fathers**' completely FREE!

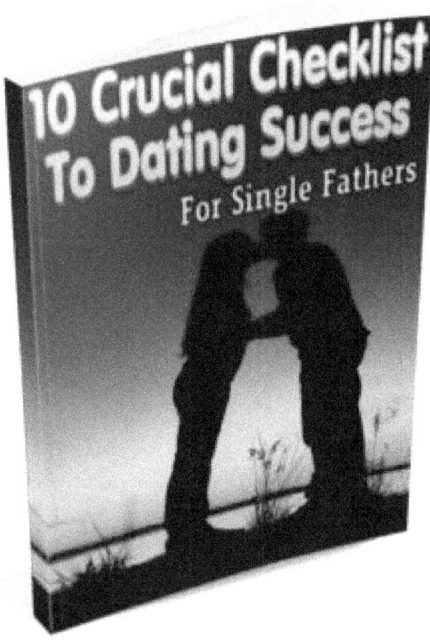

CONTENTS

Chapter 1: The House Ownership Problem

Being a single father comes with many difficulties. It is a testing period filled with trials and tribulations. Your emotional strength, parenting skills, finances and patience is being tested. Being in a single father support group, it brings me to tears when I hear some of their stories.

Their stories of financial hardship, added to their desire to provide the best for their children means they put themselves under a tremendous amount of stress. They would work hard to make things work, but there are times that they simply struggle to make ends meet.

While the difficulties facing a single parent is well-known, there isn't any reason to believe that you shouldn't realize your dream of home ownership. Thanks to the convenience of the internet together with government efforts to ensure families own their houses, it is significantly easier for you to own a home.

In recent years, the government have been coming out with guidance, financial resources and some support to ensure you would get to own your home. Getting a home is the symbol of the "American Dream".

Are you someone keen to get a home?

Getting a home is something that can be challenging because of the mortgage. When you get a home, the mortgage that you would need to pay takes up a huge chunk of your monthly income. This would really test your financial health. For many people their mortgage would take up around a third of their monthly salary. That's a huge portion, especially for a single father who needs to pay for alimony and child support.

In this book, you would learn the steps to better manage your mortgage. The key question that would be answered in this book is:

How do I save more money on mortgage repayments as a single father?

But first, I would like to go through the pros and cons of house ownership. Despite the various debates about the benefits of home ownership, there are still some disadvantages.

As a single father, getting your own home would give you a sense of accomplishment, pride and independence. Having a home you call your own gives you a feeling of comfort, that you have your future secured.

Besides that, you also set a good example to your children. You show them the value of good financial management. A home is considered an investment and you would be able to write part of your mortgage payment off on your taxes declaration. Should the value of your home rises, you would build equity and resell it in a few years' time. You would make a good profit.

Even if you don't sell it, you would keep it and slowly pay it off. Eventually, you would fully own the home. Besides these financial benefits, you can also do whatever you want to the property. Unlike a rented property, you can modify the house according to your tastes. You can plant a garden, knock down walls or whatever you can think of; because you are the owner of the property.

However, home ownership isn't all positive. There are some disadvantages too.

After you have stayed in a home you called your own for long, it would be hard for you to simply leave it. If during the custody battle it has been determined that your ex-spouse necessitate a relocation, you would need to sell the home first.

Besides that, if your working condition changes and you can't afford the home repayments anymore, you may find it difficult to sell it quickly. It gets worst if the property value actually decreases. This means that you can't even recoup the purchase price.

These are the pros and cons of house ownership.

Before purchasing a house, you should really consider all the various factors. These are important considerations because in the past few years, there have been plenty of cases of individuals who find it hard to pay their mortgages. Having to move out of your home where you and your children have a deep emotional connection is difficult.

That is where mortgage management becomes important. You need to deal with your finances well to ensure that you don't get evicted from your home should you be in a position where you can't afford the mortgage. There are many people who are paying excessive amounts of mortgage without realizing there is a way out.

From this book, I hope to share some tips given by other single fathers who have gone through what you have. It would guide you around the ways of saving more money. For me to do so, I need you to consider a few things…

Chapter 2: How Excessive Mortgage Cripple Single Fathers

For most single fathers (and two-parent fathers), mortgage is the number one expenditure that they have. A house is probably the most expensive thing you can buy in life. If it is hard for a father who has the help of his wife, it would be even more difficult for a single father who don't have anyone to help him.

If mortgage isn't managed well, it may cripple the financial health of a single father. Many single fathers in my single father support group share this same problem. They realize that they are paying a lot of money on mortgage and are looking for ways to manage this situation better.

Truth is, many single fathers aren't aware that they don't have to pay so much money on their mortgages. Because of bad financial habits and ignorance, they find themselves trapped in their mortgages. This makes their life stressful because they simply can't find a way out.

They may have delightfully sign onto the mortgage documents thinking that things won't change. The next thing they know, their working condition changes or they got a divorce. And then, they feel pressured. They find that they are tight with their finances.

Simply put, many waste their entire lifetime

paying off a mortgage, thinking they have no other choice in life. They have bought the myth of spending their entire working life paying for a mortgage.

From this book, I hope to guide single fathers who are keen to manage their mortgages better. This means having a deeper understanding of the entire house purchase process, methods of paying off your mortgage faster and having a long term plan for managing the mortgage.

Before you start to manage your mortgage, I would guide you first through the entire process before you buy a home. You would need to think about the different factors that play a role in choosing the type of home you want, the mortgage process and the closing process.

But wait, I already own a home. I already have a mortgage!

That's the thing. You need to relearn certain things. The problems that you have now would most probably be because you made some mistakes at the beginning of your home purchase. As such, it has cost you. Now, you are paying the price of such ignorance.

Understand first the considerations and then have a bigger picture of your finances. After that, you would know where to make changes in your life to reduce your mortgage and manage it better.

Chapter 3: Considerations Before Purchasing Your Dream Home

Before deciding to get a home, you need to consider if it is right for you. If it isn't, you would be better off renting. If you are a single father, you need to decide if now is the right time for you to take on a mortgage, considering you are the sole wage earner.

You only have your pay-check to consider when thinking about whether you can afford a mortgage. Besides that, it isn't only about the mortgage you need to worry about. You also need to decide on various factors that would impact the cost of home ownership.

In this chapter, you would learn about the various costs involved to home ownership besides the mortgage.

Before you start, gather a list of your income sources and amounts. Then gather the information regarding your assets and debts. Figure out how much extra money you have towards the end of the month after you have paid for all your obligations. Make sure to leave out the rental or house payment you have now.

You might want to put into considerations any potential changes regarding your finances in the near future (ideally 24 months). This may include a reduction in child support because your child would reach 18 soon. You also need to consider possible changes in your work place.

Once you have a clear picture of your finances, see if you have enough money to make this large financial commitment. Consider the following additional expenses that would impact the cost of home ownership:-

1. Insurance And Property Taxes

When you rent from others, these costs would be included in your monthly rental payments. You might not need to worry now if you are renting, but you would have to the moment you own the property.

The price for homeowners' insurance depends on where you live and which insurance company you use. The property taxes meanwhile would depend on the location that you are in. Some locations charge a higher or lower tax than others. So, keep this in mind whenever you go house-hunting.

2. Home Maintenance

As a home owner, you would need to keep your new home properly maintained. It reduces the need for spending a lot of money to pay for a large and expensive repair in the future. Routine maintenance checks should be done to ensure that unfix repairs don't get more serious in the future.

Checks like replacing roof shingles or checking for water damages can go a long way to ensure that your home is in proper condition. You can easily learn how to do some of those checks. If you don't, see if you have a friend or family member who is able to do it.

However, it pays to have an expert check it sometimes. You need to factors these costs into your home ownership. You need to put money aside towards home maintenance each month. Treat this like a 'savings account' for the house.

3. Repairs

Repairs can be a substantial cost towards your home. Before you buy a home, you would need to have it professional inspected. This home inspector would let you know about the potential large repairs that is looming in the near future. Some repairs can be so large that it wouldn't be worth it even if you get the home at half the market price.

Some issues like cosmetic issues would need to be attended to. Certain issues like old flooring, ugly wallpaper or a peeling celling would need to be addressed before you more in. Certain surprise issues can also pop up when you have already moved in. This may include fixing the water heater or electrical wiring in the home.

***

These three factors should be considered before you start purchasing a home. For single fathers who already have a home, they may realize the mistakes they have made while reading through the list.

I have known of people who forgo the professional inspection on the house, only to realize that they have spent money on a house that isn't fit for occupation. As such, they would need to spend substantial amount of money to make sure it is livable.

We have touched about your finances but I would need to go in depth about it. This would be covered in the next chapter.

Chapter 4: Have A Big Picture Of Your Finances

I have said this quite a few times in the previous few chapters: A mortgage would deeply impact your finances.

That is the reason why you need to manage it well.

Before you even think about purchasing a home, you would need to know your personal numbers well. This 'personal numbers' refer to your finances. Without understand the assets, liabilities, income and expenses that you have; buying a home can put you in a difficult position.

For a single father, he would need to consider the following before he decides to buy a new home:-

- **Alimony And Child Support.** This represents another huge chunk of expense for a single father. There are some father who pay so much in alimony and child support that it would seem impossible for them to survive if they take on a mortgage. You need to consider ways to reduce alimony and child support if your finances aren't healthy. Talk to your ex-wife about your intention to get a better home for the children. She may be willing to lower the payments if she finds that you have good intentions.

- **Food.** Food is another main cost for a single father. If your children stay with you most of the time, you should be ready for a high cost of feeding them. Growing children are constantly hungry. Even if they aren't hungry, you need to ensure that they eat regularly. You also want them to eat healthily so they grow up well.

- **Other Costs.** A single father needs to spend on other things too. This may be transport costs to go to work or utility bills to provide electricity at home. These expenses can really add up. It can be hard to have a real number to work with, but you can do some rough estimate.

- **Savings.** You can't expect to use all the excess money for the mortgage. You still need to save some money just in case something happens in the future. How much do you intend to save each month before you have the excess for mortgage payments? This would depend on your current living situation and your risk-appetite.

After considering all these costs, do you really have enough money to pay off a mortgage? You need to do a thorough check on your expenses. It pays to be detailed in this process. If it takes you some time to collect those number, do it. It pays to be accurate in such situations.

After this, you should consider ways in which you can reduce the expenses. Or perhaps, if there are other ways which you can make more money?

Instead of looking to save money, it is always better to think about the potential of making more money. This is because there is a limit to how much money you can save while the possibility of making more money is limitless.

To make more money, you need to consider areas which sucks up a lot of your time and money first. Then, look to 'save' some time first. Free up some time so that you have time to make money. You can't expect to make more money if you don't have time.

Having a big picture of your finances is important as it ensures that you don't treat the mortgage as the only thing in the world. Many people, because of their desires to own their own home, get into huge mortgages without realizing that there are other expenses to consider.

When it comes to managing your mortgage, it is important to have a long term view of your financial health. Have a strategy to make more money and to reduce your expenses. After having done this and having excess money, then only look to take on a mortgage.

Chapter 5: The Rough Process Of Buying A Home

What is the first step to take before purchasing a home?

For many people, they never think about the financial aspects before purchasing a home. They just check their eligibility and if the bank says yes, VIOLA.

They think they are ready to purchase one, without considering the reason why the bank allows them to purchase. I'll give you my unbiased opinions about banks…

Banks don't care whether you are stressed from paying bills or not. They simply want to trap you into their mortgages. If you don't pay those payments, they don't have to worry. They have the law on their side.

That is the reason why banks easily say yes to you. But a 'yes' from a bank is useless if you aren't ready. You need to remember what the hidden agenda that banks have is – they want to trap you.

Whether you have or haven't had credit problems in the past, the process of buying a home is a stressful process. It can be even worse if you are considering the purchase of a home without a partner. If you are purchasing one with a partner, at least the both of you can bounce of some ideas with each other.

Make sure to get the help or opinions of those you are close to, be it a friend or close relative. If you are looking for homes and visit a home for the second and subsequent time, make sure to bring someone else. They may be able to see certain issues that you don't. Ideally, you should get someone who isn't emotionally invested in the house as you would want him to be objective.

It is helpful to get some advice from a financial counsellor or credit adviser. They would take a real hard look of your finances. I have already gone through in depth about the importance of the 'numbers' in the previous two chapters, but getting someone professional give you advice can be helpful as well.

If you have legal obligations pertaining to your children after a divorce, it can also be helpful for you to get advice about this from your lawyer. In this chapter, you would learn in depth about the process that you can go through when evaluating your finances in depth. This should be done before you even search for a house.

Pre-Qualification Process

Once you decide that the time is right for you to own a home, you need to get yourself 'pre-qualified'. This is the time where you provide your financial documentation to prove that you have the resources available for house payment.

The lender would go through your documents to ensure its validity. After that, they would determine how much money the bank would lend to you. Remember, this is only an estimate. The actual amount of funding you may qualify for may be more or less than this amount.

You need to ask the lender about the various documents which are needed. Normally, the documents that is needed would be an identification, income verification, information on assets and debts and credit reports.

Another important aspect of this process is that your credit score and credit history would determine the interest rate for which you qualify.

The lower your interest rate, the lower your mortgage payments. That should be obvious. There are times where there are cheaper rates or special programs for single parents. Ask the banker if you qualify for such special privileges.

Looking For Home Process

The moment you have receive an estimate of the amount you qualify, you can start to go house hunting. Always remember your limit for spending and never allow the real estate agent to look for properties beyond that. Tell him that you are very firm on that.

There are some real estate agents who look to search for houses which are most expensive.

The moment you get emotionally attached to some houses, it would be difficult for you. You would purchase the house, even if it means you can barely afford it.

When finding for a home, you need to consider the various factors which are important. This may be access to school, convenience to groceries, general access and traffic. This depends on yourself and what you want.

Don't be afraid to visit a home several times to get a good 'feel' about the home. If you find that a home really suits you, you can pay a visit in the evening and at night to see what it is like.

If you feel that the home is alright, your real estate agent would go through the process of negotiation. You would also need to check that the house is inspected and appraised. Later, you would need to have the bank handle the appraisal.

This is just a rough step on the home buying process. I won't be going in depth regarding this process because this book is more about managing your mortgage, rather than the process of buying a house.

***

For single fathers who are looking for ways to manage their mortgage better, they may be struggling to understand why I have included a chapter on buying a home together with the pre-qualification process. The reason is simple: As I explain the steps better, you would be able to understand where you may have make mistakes that have cost you financially.

You can look to undo those mistakes you have made in the past. It would also help you if you decide to buy a new home in the future.

Chapter 6: Should You Pay Off Your Mortgage?

There is one question that is always been asked in personal finance.

Would it be beneficial to quickly pay down your mortgage?

Truth is, the interest rate in the past few years have been on record low. Therefore, even if you repay your mortgage as quickly as possible, you won't be able to save that much interest. Besides, you can also deduct that interest from your tax returns. What's the use of paying it off so early then?

If you are paying a high interest rate, then it pays to refinance your house. You would want to be paying less interest. For you to pay lower interest, you would need to first have a good credit rating. That is the essence of saving from your mortgage – start by developing good interest rating.

Generally, your mortgage is considered to be 'good debt'. There's a good reason for that. On average, the 30 year fixed rate is slightly above 4%. Compare that to the interest on credit card debt which is at least 10% higher, you should understand why. Credit card debt are therefore considered 'bad debt' because of its high interest.

Another thing that need to be considered when you think of paying down your mortgage is having an emergency fund. It wouldn't do you much good if you have trouble making the remaining mortgage payments should you lose your job in the future.

Ideally, you should have at least a 6 months emergency fund. This is to cover your day to day expenses if you suddenly find yourself out of job. You never know what would happen in the future.

There are some people who believe that paying down their mortgage would reduce their need for having an emergency savings. They believe that they can borrow against their home equity. However, there are some problems with such a mindset.

Over the past few years, we have seen many cases of home equity dropping. In the past, there seems to be this belief that housing prices would never drop. However, that hasn't been the case at all.

Prices has been dropping to such an extent where the value of the property even falls beyond the purchase price. As such, you should never treat your home equity as an emergency fund.

Therefore, the question of paying off your mortgage quickly should be clear. You shouldn't. The reason is that it is a good debt.

Chapter 7: Methods Of Paying Your Mortgage Earlier

In recent years, the rising cost of living has meant that many single fathers are having trouble making their mortgage payments. If you are keen to stick to a budget, you would need to take time to trim some expenses from the housing expenses.

You can easily free up some extra cash each month by reducing the monthly mortgage payment. From there, you can configure your budget to manage your monthly household expenses better. The strategies I share in this chapter would go a long way towards helping you save money on your mortgage.

- **Large Lump Sum Payment.** Making a large lump sum payment to your mortgage could help reduce the interest payment. If you happen to have a few month's bonus from the company or if you enjoy a sizeable tax refund, you can look to pay it to your mortgage. It would free up some cash in the future and reduce the debt load fast.

- **Understand Bi-weekly Payment Options.** There are some personal finance gurus who argue that making bi-weekly payments can help save you more money. It would help to pay down the mortgage faster, but beware of certain fees that could be applicable.

- **Shop Around For Better Rates.** There are plenty of lenders out there who offer better rates. You simply need to negotiate. You can even talk to your current lender about refinancing at better rates. However, you need to be careful about additional charges that come together with refinancing. It would simply cancel out any savings you have from paying lower interests. If you are someone with a good credit history, you are easily in a position to negotiate for a better rate.

- **Check Out Home Affordable Modification Program (HAMP)**. For single fathers who have problems making the mortgage payments due to their financial situation, they can check if they are eligible for HAMP. You would need to demonstrate that you have financial problems. If you are eligible, the lender would be able to modify the payment schedule to keep your budget on track.

- **Extend The Loan Life.** If you extend the

life of the loan, you would be able to reduce the monthly payments. However, you would end up paying more interest over time. This situation should only be considered if you are really struggling with cash for the next few months. However, if you have a strategy to make a big lump sum payment in the future, this could work in your favour.

Explore these various strategies to see if it would suit you as a single father. These methods should be understood in depth if you want to save money. Don't simply use these strategies but don't understand the numbers behind it!

Always check for the fine print from the bank. Very often, there are certain charges that you won't expect from the lender.

These charges can really drive up the cost of your mortgage without you realizing at all. Over time, you would end up paying even more money than you are now. Again, knowledge is power.

Chapter 8: Unusual Methods To Save On Your Mortgage

When I discussed about saving on the mortgage with other single fathers, I am surprised to hear some unusual methods of saving. I always thought that the only way to save money on my mortgage was refinancing. Boy, was I wrong.

At times, taking an unusual path to saving on your mortgage can be very smart. If you are interested in saving money, you can explore these 'methods'.

• Round It Up

By rounding up your monthly payments to the extra hundred, you can save a lot of money. Simply round up the extra 'payment' to the nearest hundred and put it to reduce your principal.

If your mortgage total is $1212.45 each month, look to pay $1300 instead. The additional $87.55 can be included to reduce the principal amount. Even if you don't round up much, the extra amount can do a lot of good that would save you interest for years. Besides that, it would also give you a psychological advantage. You feel like you are ahead of the payment schedule.

• Make 13 Payments Instead Of 12

When budgeting for each year, look to pay 13 payments instead of 12. Make this a practice each year. Force yourself to come out with the money for the additional payment.

This unusual method would work on a long term. Starting from this year, look to make 13 payments. One additional payment each year would increase the equity on your home, reduce the interest and shorten the amount of time you need to make payments.

• **Make Higher Monthly Payments**

This tip was mentioned by Rick in a single father support group meeting.

After his only son Warren has graduated and he had no other commitment, he decided to refinance his home. Previously, there was another 14 years left on his mortgage. However, he decided to refinance to paying off the mortgage in 5 years.

He had no other commitments and wanted to pay off the house fast. He could afford it and say "Why not?"

By refinancing to make higher monthly payments, you would be able to save a great deal of interests' payments. Even if might be a bit tough for the initial years, as you get your expenses tighten up, you would have a brighter future next time. Imagine the day where you have no need to pay for any more mortgage. Isn't that amazing?

＊

These three unusual methods are shared by single fathers in my support group. Evaluate their ideas and see if they are applicable to you to. These tips can go a great deal to creating more discipline in paying off your mortgage and having peace of mind.

Chapter 9: Why Your House Is A Liability

Is your house an asset or a liability?

In the world of personal finance, there is this constant debate about whether your house is an asset or a liability. For many people, their house is their number one asset. It is perhaps the biggest purchase in their lives and as such, they treat it like their most important asset.

Nothing is further from the truth, speaking from a personal finance point of view.

This goes back to your definition about what is an asset and what is a liability.

An asset is something which helps generate cash while a liability doesn't. As simple as that.

Does your house help generate cash?

If it doesn't, it is a liability. Therefore the home you stay in shouldn't be considered an asset. You should always treat the home you live in as a liability. For most people, they have this huge liability and they consider it an asset. That's why they never get ahead financially.

The bigger your house is, the higher it would cost to maintain. Think about all the costs involved in maintenance. Think of the rates, the electricity bills, water bills and the time it takes to clean the entire house. These are all 'costs' involved in having a big house.

If you are looking to get ahead financially, you

need to stop thinking that your house is an asset. Readjust that thinking and look to minimize your 'liability. This may mean living in a smaller home and reducing your housing-related costs.

From there, look to get more assets. This means investing in something else that generates cash. This is an important concept that single fathers need to embrace.

For more information about this, check out Robert Kiyosaki's book Rich Dad, Poor Dad.

Chapter 10: Look To Downsize

From the previous chapter, you should understand better why I treat the house I stay in as a liability. The other liability that many of us have is our lifestyles. For many people, they spend way too much money on things that don't matter to them. This lack of focus in spending means they 'waste' a lot of money on things.

Therefore, they need to downsize. They would have to stop spending unnecessarily. Way too many people live close to their financial limits. They take a housing loan simply because the bank allows them to and they are near their credit limits on their credit cards. Most single father never get ahead because of such thinking.

If you want to get ahead financially, you need to start living way below your limits. Then on, you can use the excess money for other things such as saving or investing. This would provide a safety blanket for both your children and yourself.

One way to downsize is to spend less than 50% of your income each month. This includes your housing costs as well. For many single fathers, this target may seem too difficult. However, they are great benefits to pushing the limits of your expenses. You would gain more freedom in the future.

If you have a lot of debt, look to reduce it first. With the excess that you save, you can slowly pay off the credit card debt. But, your housing is something that you can use to save more money. By downsizing your home, this can be easily done.

If possible, move to a smaller home. Find a home that you can easily pay off and also don't spend so much money to maintain. With a smaller home, you would incur less electricity, gas or other housing costs.

Besides having a reduced expense, you would also have less place to store material items. Many people buy many things to fill up their homes. As such, the bigger their homes, the more things they buy. Worst still, most of the things they buy are completely unnecessary.

This is when you need to think about the priorities you have. You need to be clear about the things that you value in life. For me, I value:-

- Time with my children

- Time for myself

- Pursuing my hobbies

- Having financial freedom

Wasting time to pay off a house which is too big is a complete waste. You simply waste your lifetime on something that don't matter much. Do you really need that big house?

If you are honest, the answer is NO.

You can easily life a simple life with a smaller home. You won't have to incur the crazy mortgage payments that you have to struggle for each month. I have known single fathers who work so hard to pay off their homes that they don't even have time to stay in it. How stupid can it be!

If you suddenly realize the redundancy of paying for such an expensive home, you may want to make changes in your life. I congratulate you for it.

You may decide to sell off your current home

and move to a smaller one. You may even decide to rent in the future before you find a more suitable house to purchase for your needs. By selling off your home, you can have excess money for other things like your children's future education and having more time to be with them.

What do you value in life? It is easily reflected by the home and mortgage you have.

LEAVE A REVIEW

I hope this book has helped you well. It isn't my intention at all to go deep into the topic. I am no expert in everything. However, I have the help of many other single fathers who have shared with me their invaluable experience.

If this book has helped you in any way, do leave me a review. This helps build our single father community.

If you feel that this book can be improved in any way, do mention it in the review. I would love to hear from you.

I wish you luck as a single father…

ABOUT NICK THOMAS

Nicholas Thomas has helped many single fathers cope with divorce in the past few years. By helping them gain more confidence and stability in their lives, he is able to guide them towards being a man that attracts other women easily.

He divorced back in 2008 and knows how difficult a divorce can be for a man. It was a terrible time for him when he got his divorce. He envisioned his children blaming him and not being able to spend time with him. It gave him a constant guilt trip.

Being a divorced man can be very difficult. Ever since his 'emotional recovery' from the divorce, he has helped many single fathers by advising and helping them gain confidence.

Should you want to share your story with him, you can do so at
www.singledaddydating.com/shareastory/

ALSO BY NICK THOMAS

(1) Dating After Divorce For The Single Daddy

(2) Dating Ideas For The Single Daddy

(3) How To Be An Alpha Male

(4) First Date Conversations

(5) Online Dating

(6) How To Approach Women

(7) Mature Dating

(8) Single Parent Support

(9) Coping With Divorce

(10) Parenting After Divorce

Visit www.singledaddydating.com/bookstore/

Get Your Complimentary
FREE BOOK

Join our community today and get **10 Crucial Checklist To Dating Success For Single Fathers** FREE, delivered right to your email…

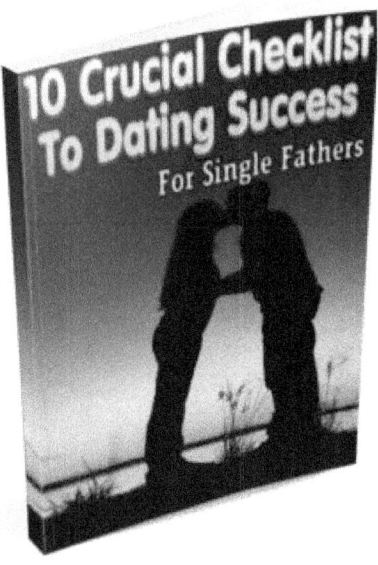

JOIN US AT
WWW.SINGLEDADDYDATING.COM/ NEWSLETTER/